C000043982

IMAGES OF WAR
THE BRITISH AT FIRST AND SECOND YPRES

RARE PHOTOGRAPHS FROM WARTIME ARCHIVES

IMAGES OF WAR

THE BRITISH AT FIRST AND SECOND YPRES

RARE PHOTOGRAPHS FROM WARTIME ARCHIVES

BOB CARRUTHERS

Pen & Sword
MILITARY

This edition published in 2015 by

Pen & Sword Military
An imprint of
Pen & Sword Books Ltd.
47 Church Street
Barnsley
South Yorkshire
S70 2AS

ISBN: 9781473836075

A CIP catalogue record for this book is available from the British Library.

Printed and bound in Malta
By Gutenberg Press Ltd

Pen & Sword Books Ltd. incorporates the imprints of Pen & Sword Aviation, Pen & Sword Family History, Pen & Sword Maritime, Pen & Sword Military, Pen & Sword Discovery, Pen & Sword Politics, Pen & Sword Atlas, Pen & Sword Archaeology, Wharncliffe Local History, Wharncliffe True Crime, Wharncliffe Transport, Pen & Sword Select, Pen & Sword Military Classics, Leo Cooper, The Praetorian Press, Claymore Press, Remember When, Seaforth Publishing and Frontline Publishing

For a complete list of Pen & Sword titles please contact

PEN & SWORD BOOKS LIMITED
47 Church Street, Barnsley, South Yorkshire, S70 2AS, England
E-mail: enquiries@pen-and-sword.co.uk
Website: www.pen-and-sword.co.uk

Contents

Chapter One
THE BEF AND THE ROAD TO YPRES **6**

Chapter Two
THE RACE TO THE SEA **30**

Chapter Three
THE YPRES SALIENT **39**

Chapter Four
THE FIRST BATTLE OF YPRES **59**

Chapter Five
THE SECOND BATTLE OF YPRES **89**

Chapter One

THE BEF AND THE ROAD TO YPRES

The photographs in this book depict the men of the British Expeditionary Force, or BEF, who, from 1914–1918, formed the garrison of the beleaguered Belgian town of Ypres and the salient which surrounded it. The BEF was the force sent to the Western Front during the opening days of the First World War. The first wave of men from 1914 who look back at us from these pages were the regular volunteers of the standing army and they represented the cream of Britain's manpower; highly trained, motivated and professional in their outlook.

Under the terms of the Entente Cordiale, the British Army's role in a European war was to embark soldiers of the British Expeditionary Force, which initially was to consist of six infantry divisions and five cavalry brigades that were arranged into I Corps and II Corps. However, the British Secretary of State for War, Lord Kitchener, believing Britain should husband her resources for a long war and guard against German invasion, convinced the Cabinet on 6 August that the initial BEF led by General French would consist of only four infantry divisions (and one of cavalry), and not the six which had been promised.

The hurried preparations for the movement of the BEF to France are brought vividly to life by the photographs in this book, which are largely drawn from contemporary periodicals. Where possible the flavour of the period has been honoured by using the original captions. This can lead to a rather jingoistic tone, but that was certainly the mood of 1914 and it seems appropriate to reflect that in these pages.

Emperor Wilhelm II of Germany, who was purportedly dismissive of the BEF, allegedly issued an order on 19 August 1914 calling on the Imperial German army to 'exterminate... the treacherous English and walk over General French's contemptible little army'. Hence, in later years, the survivors of the regular army dubbed themselves 'The Old Contemptibles'. It is important to note, however, that no evidence of any such order being issued by the Kaiser has ever been found. It was probably a British propaganda invention, albeit one often repeated as fact.

The term 'British Expeditionary Force' is often used to refer only to the forces present in France prior to the end of the First Battle of Ypres on 22 November 1914, although the more widely recognised alternative endpoint of the BEF is 26 December 1914, when, with the Ypres salient firmly established, the BEF was divided into the First and Second

Armies. However, the BEF remained the official name of the British armies in France and Flanders throughout the First World War.

In 1914 Lord Kitchener stated that the conflict would plumb the depths of manpower 'to the last million'. Against Cabinet opinion, Kitchener controversially predicted a long war that would last at least three years, require huge new armies to defeat Germany and cause huge casualties before the end would come. As a result of his realistic stance a massive recruitment campaign began to raise a new army. The activities which surrounded the raising of that army can be traced in the pages which follow. The recruiting campaign for the new armies featured the famous poster of Kitchener, taken from the 5 September 1914 *London Opinion* magazine cover (shown above right). It played its part in encouraging large numbers of volunteers and has proven to be one of the most enduring images of the war. Kitchener built up the 'New Armies' as separate units because he distrusted the Territorials from what he had seen as an observer during the Franco-Prussian War with the French Army in 1870. This may have been an erroneous comparison, as the British reservists of 1914 tended to be much younger and fitter and more courageous than their French equivalents a generation earlier.

At the War Council on 5 August 1914, Kitchener and Lieutenant General Sir Douglas Haig argued that the BEF should be deployed at Amiens near the French coast, where it could deliver a vigorous counterattack once the thrust of the German advance was known. Kitchener argued that the deployment of the BEF in Belgium would result in having to retreat and abandon much of its supplies almost immediately, as the Belgian Army would almost certainly be unable to hold its ground against the Germans. The War Council disagreed, placing their trust in the network of mutually supporting fortresses constructed by the Belgians. Kitchener's wish to concentrate further back at Amiens was overruled by the Prime Minister, who eventually agreed that the BEF should assemble at Maubeuge. It was to prove a fateful decision.

As matters developed Kitchener was proved right, and a disaster was only narrowly averted due to the grit, professionalism and endurance of the BEF. Kitchener's decision to hold back two of the six divisions of the BEF, although based on exaggerated concerns about German invasion of Britain, arguably saved the BEF from disaster as Sir John French might have been tempted to advance further into the teeth of the advancing German forces, had his own force been stronger. By the end of September 1914 – after the battles of Mons, Le Cateau and the Aisne – the old regular British Army had suffered massive casualties and lost most of its fighting strength; but it had managed to help stop the German advance. It is sobering to realise how few of the men who we see in rude health in the contemporary photographs were actually destined to survive. Regrettably, due to the refusal of the War Office to engage with the press, there are all too few photographs of the BEF from 1914; the best of those which did make it to print are featured here.

Lance Corporal C.A. Jarvis encourages potential recruits to enlist at Woodford Green recruiting station.

Eager future soldiers queue up outside an Army Recruiting Office.

Here we see members of the Territorial Force posing with an officer outside a recruiting office. The Territorial Force was formed in 1908, with the intention of providing a home defence force to bolster the regular forces of the British Army. However, many battalions served in France, having volunteered following the announcement of the First World War.

White City, 1914 – willing volunteers take the oath at the recruitment offices. Many expected that the war would be over by Christmas; the reality that awaited them would be far different.

A crowd gathers in Trafalgar Square to hear a rallying speech given by Lance Corporal E. Dwyer.

A recruit undergoes the army eyesight test. Recruits hoping to serve in the army were subjected to medical examinations designed to highlight any problems with the teeth, chest or eyesight.

Bermondsey, London – new recruits line up, ready to begin training.

Training was a gruelling process for the soldiers, often consisting of 16-mile hikes whilst carrying a rifle, the soldier's kit and roughly 60lb of ammunition. However, nothing would be able to prepare the men for the harsh realities of war in the trenches.

New recruits are accompanied by children.

Many reservists were re-called to serve alongside the French armies and the British Expeditionary Force. They were dispatched to the continent alongside five cavalry brigades.

August 1914 – the Scots Guards marching to Waterloo Station on their way to the battlefields of Flanders.

The first battalion of the Grenadier Guards marching from Wellington Barracks to Waterloo Station on its way to the front.

Here we see Westminster Fusiliers waiting at Waterloo Station for their troop train.

A troopship crossing the channel carrying horses and British troops.

Following a long journey to France, British troops seize the chance for a much needed nap on the Boulogne Quay.

British gunners ashore at Boulogne, ready for the land journey to the battlefield.

British troops line up for inspection at Havre before setting off for the front.

A rousing cheer from the men of the BEF.

22 August 1914 – troops resting in the Grand Place before the Battle of Mons. Shown here is a company of the 4th Battalion Royal Fusiliers.

Side by side, Belgian and British troops retreat, deflated, from Mons.

British soldiers, on the retreat from Mons, march alongside Belgian refugees.

Following the fall of Antwerp, wounded soldiers arrive at Ostend.

British troops pose for a photograph in a square in Belgium.

August 1914 – infantry entraining for a southern seaport.

August 1914 – the Queen's Royal West Surrey Regiment 1st Battalion before it is deployed to France.

The London Scottish were among the first of the territorial regiments to volunteer for service.

Chapter Two

THE RACE TO THE SEA

Following the German retreat from the Aisne, a series of outflanking moves were attempted by both sides which became known as 'the race to the sea'. As the opposing lines moved inexorably northwards, Flanders was to become the focal point of the war. On 27 August, a squadron of the Royal Naval Air Service flew to Ostend, for reconnaissance sorties between Bruges, Ghent and Ypres. British marines landed at Dunkirk on the night of 19/20 September and on 28 September, a battalion occupied Lille. The rest of the brigade occupied Cassel on 30 September. The RNAS Armoured Car Section was swiftly created by fitting vehicles with bullet-proof steel and the marines scouted the country in motor cars and engaged in combat with German Uhlans. On 2 October, the Marine Brigade was sent to Antwerp, followed by the rest of the Naval Division on 6 October, having landed at Dunkirk on the night of 4/5 October. These often overlooked events can also be glimpsed in these pages.

In late September, Joffre and French discussed the transfer of the BEF from the area around the Aisne to Flanders. The strategic idea was to unify the British forces on the Continent, shorten the British lines of communication from England and to defend Antwerp and the Channel ports. Despite the inconvenience of British troops crossing French lines of communication, when French forces were also moving north after the Battle of the Aisne, on the night of 1–2 October, in great secrecy, the transfer of the BEF from the Aisne front began. Marches were made at night and billeted troops were forbidden to venture outside in daylight. On 3 October, a German wireless message was intercepted, which showed that the BEF was still believed to be on the Aisne.

Men of the BEF marching away with kitbags slung over their shoulders.

A man of the Middlesex Regiment and a Yorkshire Light Infantryman were among the first casualties of the Great War.

In the wake of the German retreat, British troops search a village house by house.

British marines manning a machine-gun in an improvised position.

Two Highlanders, injured in the first great battle, returning home in a Channel steamer.

(Left) A kind-hearted British soldier gives a wounded German soldier a cigarette and a light from his pipe. (Right) These Germans had their wounds dressed in a British field hospital.

A group of the Manchester Regiment wounded in the opening battles of the war.

British marines march into Ostend.

More British marines cross the bridge and enter the town of Ostend.

The men had to carry much of their heavy equipment on the shoulder.

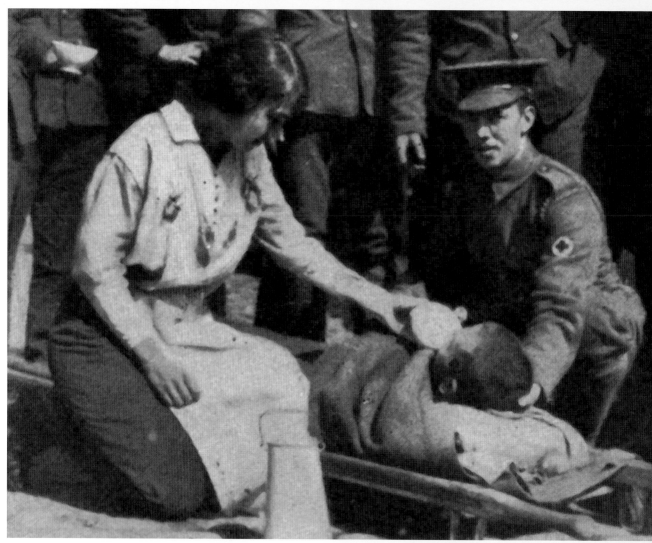

A French woman provides coffee for a badly-wounded German in the care of the Royal Army Medical Corps.

A British armoured car rumbles through the streets of Antwerp.

Chapter Three

THE YPRES SALIENT

Following the fall of Antwerp, the last major blocking position on the road to Calais was the small market town of Ypres and it was here that the BEF determined to make a stand. The Ypres Salient incorporated the area around Ypres and was destined to become the scene of some of the fiercest battles in the First World War. In military terms, a salient is a piece of friendly-held territory that bulges into enemy territory therefore, a salient is therefore surrounded by the enemy on three sides, making the troops occupying the salient especially vulnerable.

The Ypres Salient was formed by British, French, Canadian and Belgian defensive efforts against German incursion during the 1914 'Race to the Sea', culminating in the Battle of the Yser and the First Battle of Ypres. These battles were centred around Ypres but the allies were forced back on either side of the town. Ypres was located at the centre of a salient which bulged into the German lines, although the little corner of Belgium around Veurne had been saved from occupation, this was also the beginning of trench warfare as both sides 'dug in' around the line of the salient.

The terrain around Ypres is mainly meadow, cut by canals, dykes, drainage ditches and roads built up on causeways. The Lys, Yser and upper Scheldt are canalized and between them the water level underground is close to the surface, rises further in the autumn and fills any hollow in the ground, which quickly turns to a muddy morass.

In the rest of the Flanders Plain were woods and small fields, divided by hedgerows planted with trees and fields cultivated from small villages and farms. The terrain was difficult for infantry operations because of the lack of observation, impossible for mounted action because of the many obstructions and awkward for artillery because of the limited observation opportunities. The difficulty of movement after the end of summer absorbed much of the labour available on road maintenance, leaving field defences to be built by front-line soldiers.

British big guns going to the front before their deadly work begins.

The town of Ypres lay at the juncture of the British and Belgian lines.

Belgian troops, exhausted by the long retreat to Ypres, take a welcome rest.

Footsore and mud-encrusted Belgian troops plod on towards Ypres.

For a brief time Belgian guns served alongside the Royal Artillery.

Belgian troops, intermingled with British, man a hedge line near Ypres.

The British Army around Ypres prepares for the long haul by building field ovens for baking bread.

The first loaves leave the newly-prepared ovens.

This photograph gives an idea of the scale of the daily operations mounted by the commissariat.

The relentless task of feeding thousands of men was repeated every day during four years of battle.

British marines marching through the streets. They are pictured here in Ostend, 1914.

Allied troops are pictured here, putting on a brave face, in France.

8 September 1914 — at Signy Signets, soldiers from the 1st Middlesex first-line transport find themselves bombarded by shrapnel.

Lieutenant Arkwright bivouacked in the grounds of a chateau in Champs. The brave Lieutenant was later killed whilst flying in the war.

British encampment in Northern France.

Messines (about midway between Ypres and Armentières). This photograph was taken during the heavy fighting in October 1914.

General Gough at his headquarters in France. This popular cavalry commander (in the centre of the photograph) is seen chatting with two members of his staff during a lull in the fighting along the Franco-Belgian frontier. General Gough was specially mentioned in Sir John French's despatches and promoted to major-general for his distinguished service.

British lancers going into action across an open stretch of country in northern France.

A glimpse of old-world Ypres – one of the water-gates of the city, guarding a canal entrance.

The top left-hand picture shows the thirteenth-century cathedral of St Martin in flames. To the right is a photograph of the famous 'Halles des Drapiers' (or Cloth Hall), another thirteenth-century building, also set on fire by German shells. Inset is a small view of the Cloth Hall as it was; and below it, on the left, this once beautiful building as the flames were springing from tier to tier of its lovely facade. The two lower views show (left) the remains of the Market Hall and (right) the interior of the cathedral after bombardment.

Cabbages as cover – British trench dug just behind a row of cabbages. The German trenches were one hundred and eighty yards in front.

Another view behind the shelter of the cabbage-patch. British sharpshooters on the look-out for a Prussian sniper. Some of the enemy snipers dressed themselves in khaki.

Motor-bus transport for the Allied troops in Flanders. Troops were conveyed to both Ypres and Dixmude by motor-buses which used to be on service in the streets of Paris.

British soldiers preparing to leave Ostend for a new base.

An ever-welcome gift to a comrade on service – a good cigar.

A British soldier seeks expert advice on a problem in Belgian topography.

A cavalry regiment enjoying a hurried meal behind the lines prior to going into action at Ypres.

The London Scottish off-duty in France, 1914.

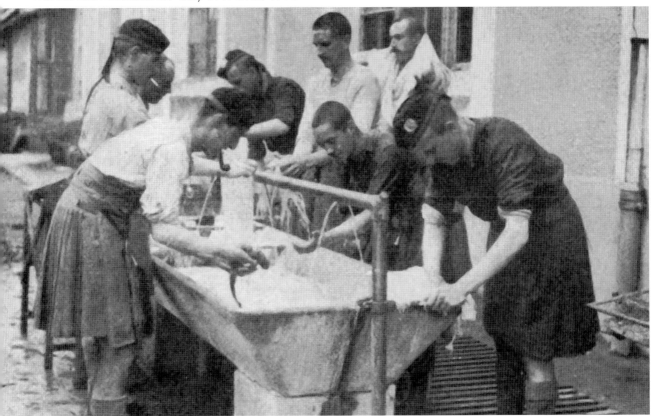

London Scottish resting at a wayside station a few days before their famous charge. The London Scots are seen enjoying an impromptu meal and a smoke at a railway station in France.

Chapter Four

THE FIRST BATTLE OF YPRES

The fighting which is collectively known as the First Battle of Ypres has been divided into five stages: an encounter battle from 19–21 October, the Battle of Langemarck from 21–24 October, the battles at La Bassée and Armentières to 2 November, coincident with more Allied attacks at Ypres and the Battle of Gheluvelt (29–31 October), a fourth phase with the last big German offensive which culminated at the Battle of Nonne Bosschen on 11 November, then local operations, which faded out in late November. During these engagements the men of the Territorial battalions, and the London Scottish in particular, distinguished themselves by their heroic conduct.

The running battles from Armentières to Messines and Ypres are best understood as a single battle in two parts. Firstly an offensive by III Corps and the Cavalry Corps which lasted from 12–18 October, forcing the Germans to retire. However, the attacks by the BEF, Belgians and a new French Eighth Army in Belgium made little progress beyond Ypres. These actions were followed by a counter-offensive by the German 6th and 4th armies from 19 October – 2 November, which from 30 October took place mainly north of the Lys, and as a result the battles of Armentières and Messines merged with the Battles of Ypres. The most famous episode took place from 21–23 October, as German reservists made mass attacks at Langemarck, with losses of up to 70 per cent with little effect as the 4th and 6th armies took small amounts of ground at great cost to both sides.

Falkenhayn then tried a limited offensive to capture Ypres and Mount Kemmel, from 19 October – 22 November. French, British and Belgian troops in improvised field defences repulsed German attacks for four weeks. In the final analysis, neither side had moved forces to Flanders fast enough to obtain a decisive victory and by November, both were exhausted, short of ammunition and suffering from collapses in morale; some infantry units refused orders. Unlike the battles of manoeuvre in the summer, the autumn battles in Flanders quickly became static, attritional operations.

The battles for Ypres were dominated by artillery and this trend was marked, in October 1914, when Kitchener forecast a long war and placed orders for the manufacture of a large number of field, medium and heavy guns and howitzers, sufficient to equip a 24-division army. The order was soon increased by the War Office but the rate of shell manufacture had a more immediate effect on operations. While the BEF was still on the Aisne front, ammunition production for field guns and howitzers was 10,000 shells a month and only 100 shells per month were being manufactured for 60-pounder guns; the War Office sent another 101 heavy guns to France during October.

As the contending armies moved north into Flanders, the flat terrain and obstructed view, caused by the number of buildings, industrial concerns, tree foliage and field boundaries, forced changes in British artillery methods. Lack of observation was remedied in part by decentralising artillery to infantry brigades and by locating the guns in the front line but this made them more vulnerable and several batteries were overrun in the fighting between Arras and Ypres. Devolving control of the guns made concentrated artillery-fire difficult to arrange, because of a lack of field telephones and the obscuring of signal flags by mists and fog.

October 1914 – soldiers from the 2nd Battalion Gordon Highlanders wait to advance at Ypres.

October 1914 – soldiers from the Oxford and Bucks Light Infantry find themselves forced to shelter from shrapnel during the First Battle of Ypres.

The all-night battle in which the London Scottish took part on 31 October – 1 November 1914, to the south of Ypres, was an event in which for the first time a complete unit of our Territorial Army fought alongside its sister units of the Regulars. These photographs show groups of the hardy Scots after their 'baptism of fire', which lasted from 9 pm til 2 am They inflicted far more damage on the enemy than they received.

October 31 1914 – pictured here we see the London Scottish after the Battle of Messines, their numbers sadly depleted.

Used up in heavy marching: discarded relics of many a weary march.

British marksmen behind a sand-bag barricade. Often the shallow nature of the ground in Flanders did not allow for effective trench-digging, and men fought from behind fortifications constructed with sand-bags and carts.

Field Marshal French makes a wayside inspection of infantry on their way to the trenches.

A British despatch-rider faces muddy conditions in rain-soaked Flanders.

British troops armed with rifle-grenades, the invention of Mr Marten-Hale.

A rest by the way – on the edge of a sheltered coppice in Flanders.

November 9 1914 – Queen's Royal West Surrey Regiment 1st Battalion.

Harnessed dogs pull a machine-gun and ammo. These weapons could weigh as much as 150 pounds.

November 1914 – 2nd Argyll and Sutherland Highlander Captain Moorhouse sniping, Bois Grenier.

German 150 mm shells burst in front of a concealed Allied battery.

British colonial volunteers with a detachment of Belgian cavalry.

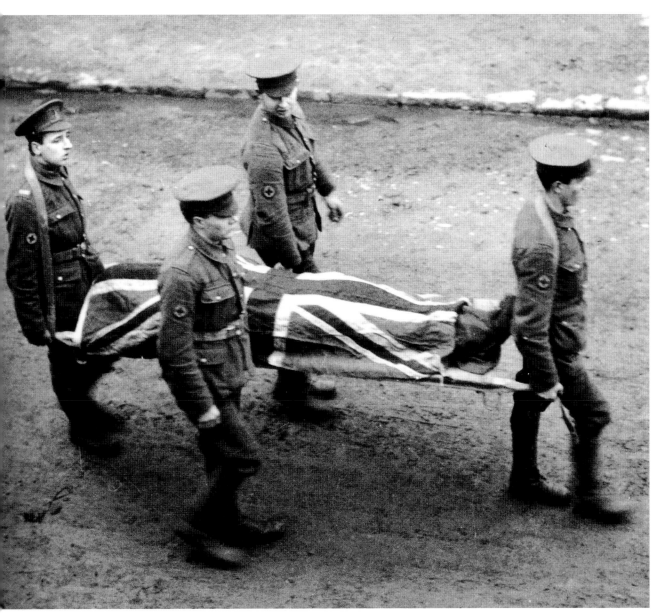

December 1914 – the funeral of a 2nd Scots Guard private, Estaires.

British colonial troops attached to the 3rd Belgian Lancers.

Men of the Cameronians' 1st Battalion in winter attire behind their snow-covered defences.

A trench occupied by Cameron Highlanders, the snow reminding them of a real old highland winter.

A remarkable photograph of a British entrenched position at the front.

Liverpool Scottish territorials in the trenches.

The distinctive coats of the Royal Scots Fusiliers are noticeable here, as we see them entrenched during the winter of 1914.

British pioneers at work with a pick and shovel.

December 1914 – British and German soldiers stand together on the battlefield near Ploegsteert.

Christmas Day 1914 – not a very merry Christmas for the 1st Battalion London Rifle Brigade at Ploegsteert Wood.

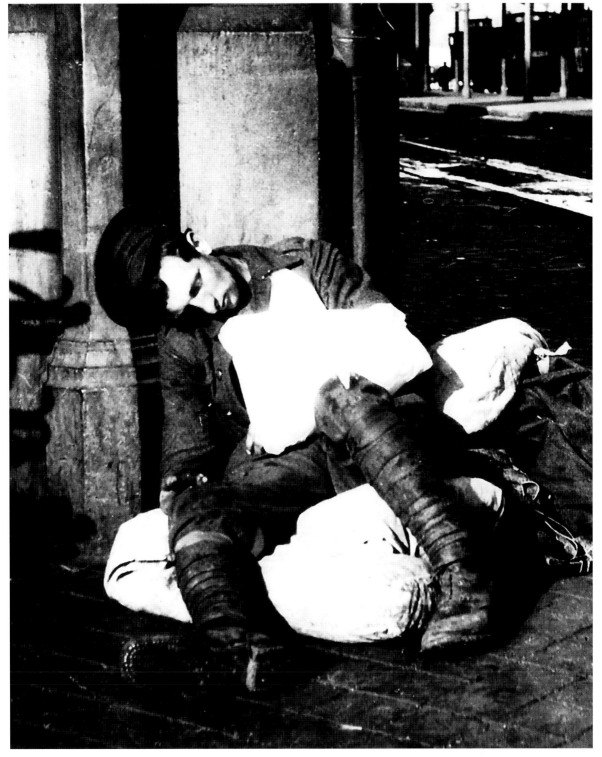

Waiting for the train home, a wounded British soldier slumps on the floor. He waits for the Red Cross and the train that will take him home for the first Christmas of the war.

March 1915 – soldiers from the Gordon Highlanders washing at Laventie.

This photograph illustrates the proximity of the conflicting armies. In the foreground is a French communication trench across a village road, with barrels on the parapets for protection against the fire of the enemy. It would have been fatal to cross the road except by means of the trench.

Allied troops entrenched at the Battle of Neuve Chappelle. The allies would suffer around 12,500 casualties.

The welcoming Belgian public surround men from the South Staffordshire Regiment.

During quieter times in the trenches infantrymen would read and smoke.

A street in shell-shattered Arras.

Graves of men of the 1st Loyal North Lancashire Regiment: a British patrol halt to do honour to the departed brave.

Chapter Five

THE SECOND BATTLE
OF YPRES

The area of the salient is mostly flat, with few rises or hills. Those that did exist became the focus for the 1915 Second Battle of Ypres, which saw the first use of gas and the almost total destruction and evacuation of Ypres. The Flanders plain is bounded by canals linking Douai, Béthune, St Omer and Calais. To the south-east, canals run between Lens, Lille, Roubaix and Courtrai, the Lys river runs from Courtrai to Ghent and to the north-west lies the sea. The plain is flat, apart from a line of low hills from Cassel, eastwards to Mont des Cats, Mont Noir, Mont Rouge, Scherpenberg and Mount Kemmel. From Kemmel, a low ridge lies to the north-east, declining in elevation past Ypres through Wytschaete, Gheluvelt and Passchendaele, curving north then north-west to Dixmude where it merges with the plain.

South of La Bassée Canal around Lens and Béthune was a coal-mining district full of slag heaps, pit-heads (fosses) and miners' houses (corons). North of the canal, the city of Lille, Tourcoing and Roubaix formed a manufacturing complex, with outlying industries at Armentières, Comines, Halluin and Menin, along the Lys river, with isolated sugar beet and alcohol refineries, and a steel works near Aire, whilst the intervening areas were agricultural.

The Second Battle of Ypres was fought from 22 April – 25 May 1915 for control of the town, following the First Battle of Ypres the previous autumn. It marked the first mass use by Germany of poison gas on the Western Front. For the first time a former colonial force (the 1st Canadian Division) defeated that of a European power (the German Empire) on European soil, in the Battle of St Julien and the Battle of Kitcheners' Wood, which were the chief engagements within the Second Battle of Ypres.

German accounts stress the accuracy of Allied sniper fire, which led troops to remove the spike from Pickelhaube helmets and for officers to carry rifles to be less conspicuous. In these pages we are privileged to have a visual reminder of allied snipers at work. However, artillery remained the main infantry-killer and it is this all-too-often overlooked arm which provided the anvil of victory.

Later in 1915 the focus shifted south from Ypres towards Loos, and despite the relentless nature of the fighting in 1916, Ypres slipped out of the headlines and would not become prominent again until the Battle of Passchendaele in 1917.

April 1915 – a Honorable Artillery Company soldier uses a box periscope in a front-line trench opposite the mound, as another reads during the Second Battle of Ypres, St Eloi.

Section of German barbed-wire entanglements rushed by the British. The passage was forced under heavy fire, indicated by the pall of smoke in the background.

British respirator parade and inspection. An addition to our soldiers' daily routine, made necessary by the poisoned-gas campaign of the enemy.

An extraordinary photograph of a rare incident. For once the Germans came out to charge a British trench, and our men are seen awaiting the order from their officer to meet the foe in the open.

In a British trench at Ypres. This photograph was taken a few moments before the order was given to charge the enemy lines.

Allied infantrymen fighting side-by-side in the trenches. On the right of the photograph a Belgian officer is seen directing the fire of his own men.

The first Territorial recipient of the VC, Second Lieutenant Geoffrey Harold Woolley, of the Queen Victoria's Rifles. At Hill 60, on the night of 20–21 April 1915, he picked up a hand-grenade which had been thrown into the trench, and before the fuse had burned to the charge threw it out, thereby saving many lives.

A scene in a village in Flanders, where a German shell had burst near a British transport wagon.

Ambulances waiting to convey wounded out of the danger zone at Ypres.

Soldiers stand in the ruins of a historic cathedral.

The three highlanders pictured withstood an attack on the convoy they were guarding by fifty Germans, killing seventeen in the process.

Beautiful carvings in a church near the British front shattered by German shell-fire.

British officer's quarters in the attic of a French farmhouse behind the firing-line.

An unexploded German shell, obviously intended for the church in the background, discovered by British soldiers in a meadow.

British soldiers at rest in a first-line trench near Ypres during a brief lull in the fighting. With their loaded rifles ready to hand, they were smoking and about to play cards, while one was preparing food.

British transport column driving through a shell-shattered village near Ypres. The streets were deserted, and scarce a house stood intact.

May 1915 – men of the 1/5th Battalion (TF) in their trench on the Ypres Salient.

9 May 1915 – men of 'C' Company, 2nd Lincolnshire Regiment shelter in a mine crater during the Battle of Aubers Ridge at Fromelles.

Night-time photo of German barrage of Allied trenches during the Second Battle of Ypres.

Soldiers had to make the best of what they had available. Here, two resourceful friends shave using water from a shell-hole.

A compassionate English soldier treats the head wound of a German prisoner of war.

16 June 1915 – in the background, the artillery marker planted atop the parapet was intended to signal to the artillery that the line had been secured during the Battle of Hooge.

Soldiers peer over the top of their trench into no-man's land.

No-man's land at Flanders.

Life in the trenches was not all action. Here we see British troops at rest.

In some rare down time, soldiers play a match of football.

British soldiers lining up for their rations. The neighbourhood of the camp was turned into a quagmire through inclement weather.

British soldiers working a light railway which they constructed in connection with their camp to facilitate transport.

A 155 mm shell which fell into a British trench without exploding.

British soldiers consolidating a newly-won position on the Western Front.

An Indian observer keeping watch on the enemy trenches with the aid of a periscope, which had been covered with twigs to give it the appearance of a small tree trunk.

A British gas bomb from 1915.

Belgian troops wearing early gas masks, 1915.

A close view of a British 'trench helmet'.

Dead German soldiers in front of the British trenches just before the great advance on Loos and Hulluch.

After the battle: the appalling aspect of a field near Loos. As far as the eye could see were shattered guns, limbers, automobiles and dead horses.

The Battle of Loos was launched on 25 September 1915, and was to destroy the Belgian town.

Two official photographs of wounded men returning to a dressing-station after an attack.

25 September 1915 – British infantry advancing through gas at Loos.

Some of the brave young men who fought so grandly at Loos and Hulluch.

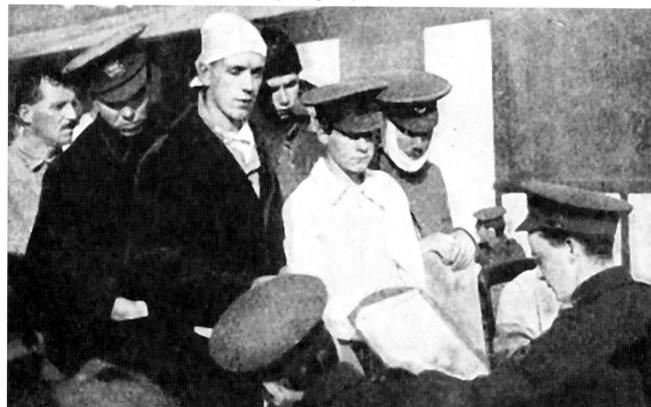

British soldiers who took part in the advance of Loos photographed at a railway station where a halt was made for refreshments during their journey home.

Captured Krupp gun which excited the interest of British and French soldiers at a railway siding in Northern France.

Autumn 1915 — battered British troops return from the Battle of Loos.

A German spy faces a British firing squad.

A welcome link to home was provided for the soldiers in the form of letters and parcels. Many of these letters are available to read today.

A kilted member of the Scottish Regiment converses with an English officer, and a private, showcasing the opposing styles of British uniform.

A new breed of headgear is tested by a Scottish infantryman. Loads of up to 60lb could be attached to the straps and carried.

Contrasting photographic views of Ypres. The photograph below was taken on 27 June 1915.

Cloth Hall in Ypres.